Do-Gooders

A Play

Graham Jones

A SAMUEL FRENCH ACTING EDITION

SAMUEL FRENCH

FOUNDED 1830

SAMUELFRENCH-LONDON.CO.UK
SAMUELFRENCH.COM

FOR AMATEUR PRODUCTION ENQUIRIES

UNITED KINGDOM AND WORLD
EXCLUDING NORTH AMERICA

plays@SamuelFrench-London.co.uk

020 7255 4302/01

Each title is subject to availability from Samuel French,

depending upon country of performance.

CHARACTERS

Nora Andrews
Tom
Simpkins
Susan
Reg
Mr Andrews, Nora's father

The action of the play takes place at Whiteside Comprehensive School and an Environmental Studies Society outing to local caves

Time—the present

CHARACTER DESCRIPTIONS

Nora Andrews A sixth form girl who tends towards idealism in her views. Intelligent, not unattractive. She would always like to please but her beliefs often prevent her from doing so.

Tom A sixth-form boy, more mature than some. More pragmatic and level-headed than Nora but not so academically bright. Good looking, amiable and amusing in a wry way.

Simpkins A young teacher with heaps of enthusiasm, some of it misplaced it is believed by some parents. Likes to be liked. Not weak-willed so much as wants to be co-operative.

Susan An attractive sixth-former, good-natured and of a happy disposition.

Reg Genial sixth-former.

Mr Andrews (*Nora's father*) Business man. In his forties. Genial but blunt at times.

AUTHOR'S NOTES

This play can be performed in any room-space. Few props are required: four chairs (not absolutely necessary); two telephones; a large map; torches; a couple of test tubes. Only some basic lighting effects are required in the cave scenes.

It is intended to be acted by young people, though there is one part (Nora's father) for a middle-aged man. The play is designed to be able to be done on minimal costs.

It is a play about pollution of our environment.

G.J.

DO-GOODERS*

Scene 1

*The sixth-form Common room of Whiteside Comprehensive School.
The stage is bare*

Two young men, Tom and Reg, enter. They are sixth-formers

Tom There's something not quite right about her in my opinion.
Reg She's very keen, that's all.
Tom Keen is right. Sometimes to the extent of being a nuisance, if
  not a pain in the neck.
Reg But I quite like Nora.
Tom I've nothing against her, except ... (*He ponders ruefully*)
Reg What?
Tom She's a bit odd, that's all.
Reg (*hesitating slightly; then decisively*) She wants me to go with
  her today.
Tom What? You're *not* going, are you, Reg?
Reg Mr Simpson says ...
Tom (*interrupting, scornfully*) Mr Simpson says! Sometimes I
  think he's as daft as Nora.
Reg He says someone ought to go with her to help out.
Tom OK. Go. Get your feet wet. Drown. But she won't get me
  going with her, you can be certain of that. The last time ...
  remember the last time?
Reg It was quite good fun.
Tom (*pointing to his neck*) I was up to here in water.
Reg I might go. I feel sorry for her. She's so ... (*searching for a
  word*) ... so ...
Tom Simple-minded.
Reg ... innocent.
Tom (*repeating, with emphasis*) Simple-minded Reg. And odd.
  How can you feel sorry for her? She's got everything.

---

*N.B. Paragraph 3 on page ii of this Acting Edition regarding
photocopying and video-recording should be carefully read.

Reg (*meaningfully*) And nothing.

Tom Oh, God, no! (*Holding out one palm*) She's got everything. (*He holds out the other palm*) She's got nothing!

Reg You know what I mean, Tom. She's quite well off. Her father runs that factory—and yet she's so ... so ... I don't know. She doesn't seem to enjoy life very much.

Tom Do you know what she is? She's one of the world's "do-gooders". And all "do-gooders" are miserable people.

Reg What's wrong with doing good?

Tom Everything. Do-gooders never want to do themselves any good, you see, only other people. Especially when other people don't want to be done good to.

Reg She's ... she's ...

Mr Simpkins, a young teacher, enters. He is carrying a test-tube with liquid in it

Simpkins Tom, Reg. Have a look at this.

Tom and Reg go to have a look at the test-tube

Well?

Tom Looks like dirty water to me.

Simpkins Reg?

Reg Definitely dirty water.

Simpkins It's from the caves.

Tom No wonder it's dirty, Mr Simpkins.

Simpkins But the water's supposed to be clean there Tom. It comes from a spring in the hills. Nora found it there.

The two boys look at each other. Simpkins does not notice the look. He is too interested in the test-tube of water

Now, when you two go with her today ...

Tom (*interrupting*) Go with her? With who Mr Simpkins?

Simpkins With Nora.

Tom I'm not going. I've got maths to do.

Simpkins I thought it was decided. She told me a couple of minutes ago that you, Tom, and you, Reg, would be going with her.

Tom Reg is going but not me. I'm sorry, Mr Simpkins, but the maths you see.

Simpkins Well I suppose it'll be all right, just the three of you and myself.
Tom Three?
Simpkins Reg, Nora and Susan.
Tom Susan?
Simpkins That's right.
Tom I didn't know Susan was going.

They look at him meaningfully

I don't really have to do the maths urgently. I could leave it until Monday or even Tuesday. (*Pausing*) I suppose I could manage it.
Simpkins You'll come then?
Tom Why not? Make a change.
Simpkins There's Nora. (*He calls*) Nora.

Nora enters

Come over here Nora. I was just showing Tom and Reg this specimen.
Nora (*effusively*) I found it near the river, where the spring water from the caves meets it. I climbed up towards the entrance to the main cave ...
Reg (*interrupting*) You shouldn't have gone there on your own Nora.
Nora Susan came with me.
Tom (*with sudden concern*) Rather dangerous for her, don't you think? (*He pauses*) For you too.
Nora She's tougher than she looks. She's got quite strong legs.
Tom Oh yes?
Simpkins I'm as excited as Nora about this find.
Nora Suppose we *do* find something wrong with the water, Reg. We can get it analysed and send it off to the Daily Voice—we might win ...
Tom (*interrupting*) What's first prize two days down the sewers of London?
Reg That's second prize—first is three days!

Reg and Tom chuckle. Simpkins at first looks blank, then laughs aloud. He likes this sort of silly banter with sixth formers. Nora smiles to please

Nora All you win is a badge.

Susan enters. She is wearing a caving helmet and carries a torch

Susan I'm ready fellers. Got my hat and my torch—'cos it'll be
dark in them thar hills.
Simpkins You look ...
Tom Very nice.

Susan smiles and looks embarrassed

Susan Are you coming with us Tom?
Tom Of course. Looking forward to it. Can't wait.

Reg gives him a look. Tom winks at Reg

Simpkins I'll just square everything with the Headmaster, then
we'll be off.

They all exit

SCENE 2

The caves

The stage is in darkness to give the effect of the caves

*Simpkins, Susan, Tom and Reg enter with torches, crawling and
walking a little when they are able*

Simpkins Hold on. Let's take a rest.

They gather round him

Where's Nora?

Nora enters with her torch

Nora (*coming up to them*) Here I am.
Simpkins Thought we'd just take a rest, Nora.
Nora But we're nearly there, Mr Simpkins.
Simpkins Are we?

*They all shine torches in the direction Nora indicates. They are
about to go when Simpkins stops them*

Hold on a while. I'm not as young as you lot. And stop calling me "Mr Simpkins" for heaven's sake—we're not in school now. Call me Ted.

Tom and Reg chuckle at this whilst Susan and Nora giggle

OK. Edward if you like. Anything but "Mr Simpkins". (*He pauses*) I'll have a fag I think. Anyone smoke?

They all indicate that they do not

Anyone mind if I do?
Nora (*quietly*) I don't think you should.

The others are embarrassed

Simpkins Don't you, Nora?
Nora Not really.

Simpkins thinks a while, then puts his cigarettes away so as not to offend Nora

Simpkins I really should try to chuck the habit. Perhaps I'd have a bit more breath left for caving expeditions like this then.
Tom Nothing wrong with the occasional fag. My grandmother smoked a pipe.
Susan (*amused*) And I suppose she lived to a hundred and ten.
Tom No. She died at forty-three. She got trapped in a cave and starved to death.

Tom and Susan both enjoy the joke

Nora A pipe isn't as bad as cigarettes.

No one responds. They feel embarrassed when Nora is in one of her "holier than thou" moods

Simpkins Where's this stream, then, Nora? Let's all go take a look at it, shall we?

Simpkins and Nora move away, stooping and crawling, and exit

(*Off*) You lot coming?
Reg I am.

Reg exits

Tom (*shouting off*) We'll stay here and think about the problems troubling mankind today!

Tom and Susan make themselves as comfortable as they can

Susan I'm glad you decided to come with us Tom. I wasn't too keen to go with Nora on my own.

Tom Why not—need I ask?

Susan She rushes about so much. She's so enthusiastic and . . .

Tom Intense.

Susan But she's such a good friend to me, Tom.

Tom She *is* intense though.

Susan She's so serious about everything.

Tom Right. Take that business about smoking just then. I mean, if people want to smoke then let them. That's what I say anyway. But not Nora, not her. She has to censor and advise and moralize. I felt really embarrassed when she told Ted not to smoke. It's not that I don't like her. It's just that I find her a bit . . .

Susan Intense.

Tom Exactly. But there's something more than just intensity. She's willful, if you know what I mean.

Susan Oh yes, I do.

Tom She's determined to change the world.

Susan (*wondering if Tom is being entirely serious*) She won't change the world in a small town like ours. What's here to change but a few shops, a couple of small industries, umpteen pubs and a few more houses?

Tom (*shrugging; trying to explain*) People like Nora go through life as if they have a mission. They're not like you or me. They're never contented. And they can't rest until they've made everyone else discontented. And it's done for the most high-minded of reasons.

There is a sound of a splash as though someone has fallen in the stream

Susan What's that?

Susan and Tom stand up as best they can and look towards the torchlights coming towards them

Simpkins enters, together with a soaking wet Reg

Tom What happened?

Simpkins Reg fell in the stream.

Tom tries to control a laugh

Tom I'm sorry Reg, but you look …
Reg I'm wet through. And cold.
Simpkins We'll have to get back and get Reg into some dry
  clothes.
Tom (*chuckling*) God, you look a sight! How did you manage it
  Reg?
Reg I slipped.
Tom Did you go under?
Reg Right under. (*He gulps*)
Simpkins Come on Reg. This way.

  Nora enters and joins the group

Nora What about the specimens, Mr Simpkins?
Simpkins Never mind about those now, Nora …
Nora I managed to get two test-tubes full …
Simpkins Good, but … .
Nora I wish we could stay longer.
Tom (*peeved*) Why don't you stay then?

Susan nudges Tom

Tom (*only to Susan*) But it's typical of her—she's got her head in
  the clouds.
Susan (*looking up*) In this place?

  *Tom chuckles. Everyone puts their head down and start crawling
  to the exit. Nora follows reluctantly with her test-tubes*

Black-out

SCENE 3

The Common Room

*Simpkins and Nora enter. He is carrying a large map which he
spreads out on the floor. They both kneel down and look at it*

Simpkins (*pointing*) That's where the stream starts. The source of
  the spring must be somewhere here.
Nora (*pointing*) Here I should say.
Simpkins Mmm. Yes. Possibly.
Nora What's that?

Simpkins Where?
Nora There.
Simpkins Buildings of some kind. Houses?
Nora Too big surely.
Simpkins A factory?
Nora Yes.

Tom enters, with his hands in his pockets

Tom What have you got there?
Simpkins (*looking up*) It's a detailed map of the area hereabouts.
  Look Tom, you can see exactly where we were the other day.
Tom No thanks, Ted. Don't mention that place to me.
Simpkins It was good fun, Tom.
Tom I know it was. Susan's got a cold. Reg has got a cold, too,
  only it might be pneumonia, and I've got a sore head where I hit
  it on the roof a couple of hundred times.
Simpkins (*laughing*) Rubbish, Tom, rubbish. (*He points at the
  map*) There Nora, that's where I think the spring originates.
Nora (*excitedly*) I believe you're right.
Tom Find anything in those tubes of water Nora?
Nora Nothing interesting I'm afraid.
Tom Just dirty water!

*Nora and Simpkins are not too interested in what Tom has to say at
the moment. They are engrossed in looking at the map*

  What do you hope to find there?

There is no reply

  (*Coming closer*) Suppose you do find something nasty.
Simpkins Mmm?
Tom I mean, you may win a prize from the Daily Whatever—a
  holiday for two in Greenland or something.
Simpkins (*pleasantly*) Yes, that's right.
Tom On the other hand you may put the cat among the pigeons.
Simpkins (*looking up*) Pigeons?
Tom Suppose the water is contaminated.
Simpkins Go on.
Tom It won't come from the spring will it?
Simpkins So?

Tom So. (*He pauses*) If not from the spring then where does it . . . would it, come from?
Nora (*rather complacently*) That surely is the object of the exercise, Tom.

Simpkins and Nora turn their attention back to the map. Tom shrugs and is about to move away when he catches sight of something on the map. He indicates something with his toe

Tom What's that there?
Simpkins Factories.
Tom Thank goodness there is nothing wrong with the water if that's the case. I wouldn't like to see that factory (*indicating with his foot again*) having to close down. After all, Nora, your father's a big noise there isn't he?

Nora shrugs. Simpkins looks thoughtful. Tom moves to leave again then remembers something

Oh, by the way, Ted, the Headmaster wants to see you.

Simpkins gets up quickly

Simpkins Now?

Tom looks at his watch

Tom (*smiling apologetically*) About five minutes ago actually.

Simpkins exits hurriedly

Tom is about to leave as well but decides, almost reluctantly, to stay

It's a relief that you found nothing, Nora. I mean, that factory where your father is a big noise . . .
Nora (*irritably*) Oh, don't go on about him, Tom.
Tom I'm not going on about him particularly, only the factory.
Nora What about the factory?
Tom It's one of a multi-national group.
Nora (*shrugging*) So?
Tom So, if there were something discovered there, something that contaminates the water then it's quite possible that the same something might be contaminating the water all over the world where the multi-national company has similar factories.

Nora is not quite so complacent now

Which makes me glad that we didn't actually discover anything
   . . . sinister.
Nora (*in a low, unenthusiastic tone*) I suppose so.
Tom I know I'm boring you to the back teeth . . .

Nora stands up, shocked that her attitude might have insulted him

Nora No you're not, Tom. Really. You're talking very good
   sense. (*Suddenly*) Gosh!
Tom What?
Nora I've sent a sample away to be analysed.
Tom Where?
Nora My uncle's lab.

Nora seems a bit embarrassed. Tom coughs in a "posh" way

He does research at a university.
Tom (*sarcastically*) Oxford or Cambridge?
Nora Neither. I don't know why I have to be so defensive.
   Durham if you want to know.

Tom shrugs

I can't help it if my father is, as you so graphically put it, "a big
   noise" in Kleyes factory. It's not something I'm particularly
   proud of. But I don't see why I should feel ashamed of it, either.
Tom Who's said anything against it?
Nora You think I'm . . . you all think it . . .
Tom What do we all think you are, Nora?
Nora Privileged in some way. Don't you, Tom?
Tom (*vaguely*) No.
Nora I'm not a good mixer. My father tells me that, so you
   needn't shake your head, Tom.

Tom shrugs. He would like to leave but he feels he can't

I hurt people's feelings.
Tom You've never hurt mine.
Nora Perhaps that's because . . . (*She hesitates*)
Tom Go on, say it. Because I'm too thick-skinned.
Nora No . . .
Tom Why should I care?
Nora I didn't mean . . .
Tom You might have hurt Ted's feelings, though.

Nora Ted? Mr Simpkins? When?

Tom There ... "When"! You don't remember do you?

Nora I *don't* remember saying anything to him to hurt his feelings.

Tom You pulled him up about his smoking.

Nora That! He didn't mind that. Anyway I was right.

Tom Of course you were right. That's the point. You *were* right. Which is why he put his cigarettes away.

Nora (*puzzled*) I don't get it, Tom.

Tom I thought you wouldn't somehow.

Nora Honestly, Tom, I don't.

Tom shrugs and appears to be leaving. Nora rushes to him and grabs his arm

Please Tom, tell me what I did that was so wrong?

Tom (*quite passionately*) You weren't wrong Nora. You were right. But if people want to smoke cigarettes and kill themselves in the process then that's their affair. It's their own lives they're destroying, not yours or mine ...

Nora But ... (*She hesitates*)

Tom What?

Nora But one has a duty ...

Tom (*interrupting*) "One" hasn't. *You* think you have.

Nora is obviously shaken as she is unable to understand how her attitude can offend. She looks crestfallen

(*Sympathetically*) Now I've hurt *your* feelings.

Nora It's just that ...

Tom ... you know you're right.

Nora ... just that ...

Tom Forget it Nora, just forget it. I'm probably talking through the back of my head anyway. How many high grades in examinations did I get last year and how many did you get? You got umpteen and I got three.

Nora It doesn't mean anything, Tom.

Tom Compared with you I'm stupid, so don't take any notice of me.

Nora Don't be silly.

Tom At least I don't smoke, so I can't be completely stupid.

They both smile

Simpkins enters looking a bit low in spirits

Simpkins Shall I take the map back, Nora?

Nora That's all right Ted, I'll take it back. (*She folds it up and is about to leave*)

Simpkins (*embarrassed*) Oh, by the way, Nora . . . both of you . . . (*coughing nervously*) . . . about this "Ted" business. I'm afraid it'll have to be Mr Simpkins from now on. For a while at least.

Tom Headmaster been getting at you?

Simpkins He doesn't approve. Too familiar.

Nora I'll return the map then . . . Mr Simpkins.

Nora exits with the map

Tom Funny old bird, the Headmaster!

Simpkins He's all right, I suppose.

Tom Been on the carpet, Ted? I'm sorry, Mr Simpkins.

Simpkins Ridiculous isn't it? Two fellows like us having to . . . The trouble is, Tom, I'm on a sort of probation year, and the Headmaster isn't too sure if he can keep me on next year.

Tom So you have to "stick to the straight and narrow", Ted. I mean—Mr Simpkins.

Simpkins For God's sake—"Ted". (*Irritably*) People have been complaining. Parents! (*Shrugging*) Some of them don't like the way I do things.

Tom They prefer the old traditional style perhaps. Chalk and talk with everybody strapped down to their desks!

Simpkins Something like that. Damn. Damn. Then there's this business of General Studies and the environment and so on. And sex.

Tom Sex?

Simpkins One of the parents maintains that I positively encourage lax sexual behaviour.

Tom I'm all in favour myself!

Simpkins (*smiling*) I know! So am I! Perhaps that's the trouble. Perhaps I am a bit lax. The thing is, Tom, I try to treat you all like sensible human beings with enquiring minds. I don't think I should encourage the closed mind, do you?

Tom Certainly not.

Simpkins I want to make people think about all the things that *should* concern them. Know what I mean? So I suppose I am a bit lax. I mean, I try to encourage discussion on everything from politics to sex. That's another thing. Politics. The Headmaster has had another complaint. This time about my political beliefs. For some reason he thinks I'm a Communist.

Tom Oh yes?

Simpkins *You* don't think I am, do you, Tom?

Tom Well . . . no . . . I mean . . .

Simpkins God! Even you!

Tom I always thought you a bit radical, Ted. . . . Er . . . sorry. "Mr . . ."

Simpkins (*firmly*) Ted. Ted. Radical yes, but I haven't got a closed mind Tom.

Tom And Communists have.

Simpkins Exactly. (*He takes out a cigarette and casually offers one to Tom*)

Tom No thanks.

Simpkins (*lighting his cigarette*) Then there's that caving expedition we went on.

Tom I thought things went reasonably well myself.

Simpkins A fiasco.

Tom I wouldn't say that . . .

Simpkins Reg's mother has been on the phone. "Why can't teachers take more care of the children in their charge", sort of thing.

Tom These things happen.

Simpkins I took him home as quickly as I could.

Tom You did the right thing Ted.

Simpkins (*smiling*) I'm glad I've got someone on my side anyway. (*He chuckles*) On the one hand there was Reg drenched to the skin, gulping for breath, and on the other there was Nora, test-tube in hand, complaining that we were leaving too soon.

They both laugh

Tom She's a fanatic, that's her trouble.

Simpkins She certainly is. (*He looks at his cigarette, then at Tom*) Perhaps I'd better get shot of this! (*He stubs it out*)

Tom Don't let Nora get to you as well Ted.

Simpkins She's right though. And I must try to give it up one of these days.

Tom Make sure the decision is yours Ted.

Simpkins Mmmm? Oh yes.

They exit

Black-out

SCENE 4

Nora enters reading a letter

Nora (*to herself*) Nothing? (*Reading*) Nothing. Good.

Susan enters briskly carrying a sheet of paper and a biro

Susan I've been looking for you. Here, sign this.
Nora What is it?
Susan A petition on behalf of Ted.
Nora Mr Simpkins!
Susan Ted.
Nora What for?
Susan Haven't you heard? They're thinking of getting rid of him, firing him.
Nora I heard something.
Susan Well, sign then.
Nora Is there any need to?
Susan Of course there is.
Nora I don't know if it's any of our business, Susan.
Susan (*peeved*) You're always going around with one petition or another Nora. Now, when it comes to something important like whether Ted stays or goes you hesitate. I don't understand you Nora, I really don't. Don't you want him to stay?
Nora Yes, of course ... but ...
Susan But what?
Nora He is only on probation.
Susan (*taken aback even more*) Nora! You come round the school with petitions to ... to save wild animals in Africa, the elephant in India, the tiger, the wolf, the bear ... then there was your petition to stop the Brazilian Government destroying the forests or some such thing ... then there are whales and porpoises and seals and gold fish ...
Nora Not gold fish Susan!
Susan Or whatever! But when it comes to saving poor Ted you won't sign.
Nora I will sign then.
Susan (*taking the paper away*) I'm not forcing you to sign.
Nora I will sign.
Susan Do you want to?

Nora (*hesitating*) All those petitions I bring around on various occasions, Susan, are important matters . . .
Susan So is this.
Nora I know. But not *so* important. But I will sign. I want to sign.

Susan allows her to sign

Susan Thanks. (*About to leave*) See you.
Nora Nothing found in the water.
Susan What water?
Nora The water we found in the cave.
Susan Oh that!
Nora It is rather murky though. I wouldn't like to drink it.
Susan Who would?
Nora It's supposed to be spring water.
Susan How are you so sure there's nothing in it?
Nora I sent it away to be analysed.

Susan stops and looks concerned

Susan Reg isn't very well.

Nora is engrossed in her letter and is not paying much attention to Susan

Do you feel like going round to see him tonight?
Nora (*looking up*) Mmm? Who?
Susan You've got your head in the clouds again, Nora. Reg. He's not well.
Nora What's wrong with him?
Susan Don't know. Tom said he didn't like the look of him when he saw him last night. He hasn't been right since that caving expedition—ever since he fell in the stream.

Susan exits

Nora stands a while in thought. Then she exits

SCENE 5

Nora enters with her father, Mr Andrews

Andrews The idea is preposterous, Nora. You're not talking about some small, insignificant company but . . .

Nora A big multi-national!

Andrews There's no need for that sneering tone.

Nora I wasn't sneering, Father.

Andrews Even if we were a small company we still couldn't halt production over a . . .

Nora I didn't ask you to halt production.

Andrews What else?

Nora Just that some sort of investigation be made . . .

Andrews Because a friend of yours is ill!

Nora As a result of falling in the stream . . .

Andrews This is crazy. If you weren't my daughter I wouldn't listen to this nonsense any longer.

Nora looks hurt

> (*Gently*) Listen to me, Nora. The sort of investigation that would have to be made would cost thousands, if not millions, of pounds. This boy . . . this friend of yours who is ill—he could be ill for all sorts of reasons. (*Pausing*) Couldn't he?

Nora sulks

> You've had the water analysed.

Nora (*looking straight at Andrews*) I don't believe that Uncle George looked hard enough. Perhaps he did the analysis just to please me. Perhaps he missed something.

Andrews He did a proper analysis.

Nora How do you know?

Andrews He told me.

Nora Have you spoken to him?

Andrews Yes.

Nora When?

Andrews A couple of days ago. Why?

Nora You haven't spoken to him for years. Did you phone him?

Andrews Yes.

Nora To find out about the sample I sent him!

Andrews No. Why should I want to know. I've got better things to do with my time. Naturally we talked about that too in passing and he said he'd found nothing.

Nora I don't believe he even looked.

Andrews (*angrily*) This is getting out of hand. What's going on in that school? You're there to be educated not to spend your time

messing about in caves with some whizz-kid of a young scatter-brained teacher. Teacher? Some teacher!
Nora (*tearfully*) He's a good teacher ...
Andrews He's a left-wing radical.
Nora I don't know what he is ...
Andrews He's a subversive influence. He's filling your head with all these idealistic notions ...

Nora starts to cry and Andrew takes hold of her

Nora. Listen to me. There's only the two of us since your mother died. I'm doing my best for you. You know that, don't you?
Nora Yes.
Andrews I've done my best to bring you up. In a way you took your mother's place. Perhaps you've had to grow up too quickly, I don't know ... But you have to learn to give and take a bit, Nora. You mustn't just see only one side of things. Try to see my point of view as well.

Nora stops crying and looks at Andrews

Nora What do you want me to do?
Andrews Nothing. Just get down to work for your examinations. And don't worry. Things will work out all right in the end. Trust me. (*He looks at his watch*) I have to go. See you tonight.

Andrews exits

Nora stands there a while, then takes out the letter from her uncle and tears it up

Nora exits

Black-out

SCENE 6

Tom, Susan and Nora enter. Tom is amusing them by demonstrating to them his inability to spell properly

Tom "Pleasure"—pleshur.
Susan I don't believe it Tom.
Tom "Anticipate"—antissipate.

Nora You never were as bad at spelling as that Tom.

Tom I was. Always. Which is why I'll never pass my English exam.

Susan How many times have you tried?

Tom Coming up for the fifth.

Nora Why don't you get someone to coach you?

Tom Ted was going to but he's not certain he'll be here for much longer.

Susan I think it's a disgrace. I think he's one of the best teachers on the staff.

Tom A lot of good that petition of yours did.

Susan It still might help. The trouble is too many parents complained about him.

Nora looks embarrassed

You needn't feel embarrassed, Nora, your father wasn't the only one to complain—mine did too.

Tom What about?

Susan His ideas on sex.

Tom Perhaps they thought you learned too much!

Nora I didn't think my father would complain but he did.

Tom I'll be sorry to see Ted go, if he does have to.

Simpkins enters

Simpkins Thanks, Tom.

Tom (*tongue in cheek*) I mean "Mr Simpkins".

Susan and Nora smile but Simpkins does not. He is evidently upset about something

What's the matter Ted? Had the push?

Simpkins No. (*He pauses*) It's something else. (*He tries to avoid looking at them*) I called in ... on my way to school ... (*He pauses and then looks at them*) Reg—he's dead.

They are all stunned into silence. Susan starts to cry

I don't know what to say. I wish I ... I have to go. Things to do. (*As he leaves*) I'm sorry ...

Simpkins exits

Susan rushes off

Tom Reg? Dead? It's not possible!

Nora stands pondering for a moment, then exits

Black-out

SCENE 7

Tom and Nora enter

Tom I can't believe your uncle wouldn't have done the analysis, Nora, if he told you he had.

Nora I don't believe he thought it important. But there's something else. My father—I think he telephoned my uncle and told him not to do it.

Tom Why should he do that? Have you quarrelled with him?

Nora We've always got on so well together, but recently ... it's since I've taken an interest in that spring water, you see. (*She pauses*) I'm going to ask someone else to make an analysis of the water.

Tom What about your father?

Nora I'm not going to tell him.

Tom Do you think you should?

Nora Of course I should Tom. Reg is dead and no one seems to know how he died.

Tom Pneumonia.

Nora They're not sure.

Tom He had the usual symptoms.

Nora So did all those people who died of Legionnaire's Disease. I think it's time we took some positive action Tom. Don't you?

Tom I'm not sure.

Nora All I'm going to do is get the water analysed. *Then* we'll have to decide what to do next.

Tom He could have picked a virus up anywhere. There's no proof he caught it from the water in the cave.

Nora Well, I'm looking for proof.

Tom And if you find "proof" that there's something in the spring water, it's still not proof that it's in the water that comes from the factory.

Nora I don't care where it comes from, if it's there at all. Do you think I *hope* there's something wrong with my father's factory? I

love my father. He's the only person I've ever loved. But . . . (*She falters*)
Tom But you have a duty.
Nora Something like that.

They exit

Black-out

SCENE 8

Simpkins, Tom, Susan and Nora enter carrying chairs for a meeting. They arrange them in a half-circle and sit down

Simpkins I don't want to make this meeting too formal . . .
Tom What's it about?
Simpkins Something's come up about us, about our society. It looks as though there isn't going to be an "Environmental Studies" Society any more.
Tom The Headmaster put the clampers on it?
Simpkins Not exactly. He's been a bit critical of course . . .
Tom (*ironically*) Of course!
Simpkins Perhaps we have been a trifle carried away.
Tom How's that, Ted?
Simpkins In various ways. (*He coughs nervously*) "Ted" for example. (*Quickly*) I mean, I don't mind, Tom, honestly. But the Headmaster could be right on . . . some things. In a way, you see.

Tom doesn't know what to say. They all shuffle uncomfortably in their seats. Simpkins is the most uncomfortable. Nora, however, is confident that what she has done all along was right. She stares hard at Simpkins but he does his best to avoid her gaze

Simpkins Other children, younger children, hear you calling me Ted and then . . . well, discipline, you see, lapses as a result.
Susan I can understand that.
Simpkins (*encouraged to go on*) There're other things. The caving business for example. That, of course, turned into a fiasco.
Nora I thought it was a success. I think . . .
Simpkins Whatever. We have to call it a day with the Society. Orders I'm afraid. (*He pauses*) So!

Tom Short meeting then!
Susan (*getting up*) I might be able to get in a game of badminton
    after all.
Tom That's not a bad idea.
They get ready to leave

Nora I'm not leaving things in the air as they are.

There is silence as they all look at Nora

    I want to organize another visit to the cave.
Simpkins (*firmly*) Can't be done, Nora.
Nora What was it that killed Reg?
Simpkins There's no reason to suppose ...
Tom You are the only one who believes that ...
Nora All we have to do is go together to the cave and take a few
    more samples of the water in the stream and get it properly
    analysed, that's all.
Tom No one wants to be bothered any more, Nora. Don't you
    realize that we're becoming a bit of a laughing stock?
Nora I don't care.
Susan Tom's right, Nora. I'm off to play badminton.

    Susan exits

Tom I might get in a hand of bridge.
Nora (*grabbing Tom's arm*) Tom.
Tom What?
Nora Won't you help?
Tom I'd like to but ... if the stream is contaminated, then so
    what?
Nora But Reg ...
Tom Reg is dead.
Nora The stream must go somewhere, Tom.
Tom Into the sea.
Nora Tom, you said yourself that if this factory is contaminating
    the stream then, who knows, possibly all the other factories like
    it, all over the place, are contaminating streams ...
Tom It's not possible.
Nora You said so yourself.
Tom I've changed my mind. People would have found out about it
    by now. And the multi-national companies, Nora, aren't as
    uncaring as all that. It's pie in the sky. You've been carried away
    by the romance of it, Nora, that's all.

Nora Romance? What's romantic about it?

Tom I don't want to talk about it any more. I want to play bridge.
(*He turns to leave*)

Nora All I'm asking is that you come with me to the cave. If I go
alone no one will believe me; they'll think I've purposely
contaminated the water.

Simpkins I'm afraid the cave is out of bounds.

Nora Do you mean the Headmaster has ...

Simpkins Not the Headmaster. The factory. Kleyes no less. They
own the land.

Nora But it's common land. That's why they call the field "the
common field".

Simpkins It might once have been, but not now, not anymore.

Nora is dumbfounded

So ... meeting closed I suppose. (*He makes to leave but stops*) By
the way, the Headmaster has decided to keep me on for another
term.

Tom That's good.

Simpkins I'm pleased about it. Not too easy to get jobs these days.

Simpkins looks at Nora but she doesn't congratulate him

Anyway, things haven't worked out too badly after all.

Simpkins exits

Tom Coming?

Nora Where?

Tom Anywhere. Take the chairs back.

Nora I don't know.

Tom What don't you know? (*He picks up two of the chairs*)

Nora (*scornfully*) If I feel like carrying chairs.

*She picks up the other two chairs and angrily strides off followed
by Tom*

Black-out

SCENE 9

Nora and her father enter. She is grim and silent. He is angry

Andrews I won't allow it. Do you hear? I thought you'd come to your senses at last. But no. You still have this ridiculous notion to pry into concerns that are no business of yours. All right. So you say it's everybody's business. And I know what you mean by that. But do you think we who are employed by Kleyes are completely stupid? Do you imagine we don't see the dangers in certain practices? Do you think we just let things go on regardless of the consequences? Do you think that because we are in business we have no conscience? (*He pauses*) Well?

Nora I don't know what to believe any more.

Andrews You accuse me of preventing you from going to the cave to get more samples. Well it's true, but not for the reasons you suppose. It's because we can't let people mess about like this. Just anybody. Cranks. The Board can't be involved with cranks. If you were a bona fide member of some respectable organization it would be different.

Nora We had a "respectable" society in school until pressure was put on Mr Simpkins to stop it. Now there's no society any longer. Now I'm on my own.

Andrews On your own? Do you realize what being on your own does for me? It makes me look like a laughing stock. I can't even run my own household let alone a thriving business!

Nora I'm sorry ...

Andrews You're sorry!

Nora I'm sorry but I think it's important ...

Andrews (*losing his temper*) Nonsense. I won't have it. I won't tolerate a daughter of mine ...

Nora breaks down in tears

Listen to me, Nora. Listen to common sense.

Andrews tries to take Nora in his arms to console her but she pulls away from him

Nora rushes off

Andrews follows her, dejectedly

Black-out

SCENE 10

Andrews is making a phone call on one side of the stage. Susan answers it on the other side

Susan (*on the phone*) Hello?

Andrews (*on the phone*) I wanted to speak to Mr Simpkins.

Susan (*on the phone*) You've come through to the Common Room but I did see him in the corridor a minute ago. I'll go see if he's still there. Who's speaking please?

Andrews (*on the phone*) Mr Andrews, Nora's father.

Susan (*on the phone*) I'll see if he's there ...

Susan exits and returns with Simpkins

Simpkins (*on the phone*) Hello? Mr Andrews?

Andrews (*on the phone*) I'm a bit worried about Nora. I've just spoken to the Headmaster and he said he'd put me through to you ...

Simpkins (*on the phone*) He guessed I'd be here ...

Andrews (*on the phone*) Is she in school?

Simpkins (*on the phone*) I haven't seen her today yet. ... Just a moment. (*To Susan*) Susan, have you seen Nora today?

Susan No.

Simpkins (*on the phone*) A friend of hers hasn't seen her either today.

Andrews (*on the phone*) She left home this morning earlier than usual.

Simpkins (*on the phone*) She's probably around here somewhere ...

Andrews (*on the phone*) We had a bit of a bust-up yesterday about that contaminated water business, you see. She was upset. I was a bit hard on her. I feel sorry about it now but yesterday it seemed to me that things had got right out of hand.

Simpkins (*on the phone*) As far as I'm concerned the matter's dropped.

Andrews (*on the phone*) And for that I'm grateful ...

Simpkins (*on the phone*) I wonder!

Andrews (*on the phone*) What's that?

Simpkins (*on the phone*) I've just had a thought. Could you hold on a minute please?

Andrews (*on the phone*) Of course.

Simpkins (*to Susan*) Have you seen Tom this morning?
Susan No, not this morning.
Simpkins Mmm. So Tom's not here either!
Susan What do you think?
Simpkins I don't know what to think. Except ... (*into the phone*) Mr Andrews?
Andrews (*on the phone*) Yes?
Simpkins (*on the phone*) I'm wondering ... I can't believe they would ...
Andrews (*on the phone*) What?
Simpkins (*on the phone*) Your daughter had become ... how can I put it? ...
Andrews (*on the phone*) Forget the delicacy now, Mr Simpkins.
Simpkins (*on the phone*) She'd become quite fanatical about certain ideas.
Andrews (*on the phone*) That's true.
Simpkins (*on the phone*) Do you think she might have gone back to the cave for more samples?

Silence. There is a pause whilst Mr Simpkins and Susan wait for Andrews to consider this idea

Andrews (*on the phone: crestfallen*) Yes, that's where she *must* have gone. But the place isn't safe.
Simpkins (*on the phone*) Safe as houses, Mr Andrews, believe me.
Andrews (*on the phone*) I mean the water.
Simpkins (*on the phone*) What about the water?
Andrews (*on the phone*) The boy who fell in the stream! It could happen again. I'm going there now.
Simpkins (*on the phone*) So am I.

Andrews and Simpkins replace their respective receivers

Everyone exits

Black-out

SCENE 11

The caves

The stage is in darkness again to represent the caves. Andrews,

Simpkins and Susan enter, groping their way into the cave with the help of torches

Andrews (*calling*) Nora.
Simpkins This is the way. Not far now to the stream.
Andrews (*calling*) Nora. Are you here?
Simpkins You try Susan.
Susan (*calling*) Nora. Tom. It's me Susan.

> *Torches can be seen from the other side of the stage. Tom and Nora emerge from the darkness. They both have samples of the water in test-tubes*

Andrews Nora?
Nora Yes. What are you doing here, Father?
Andrews I was worried about you. Are you all right?
Nora Yes.
Susan Tom?
Tom I'm here. I decided to come with her. Somebody had to.
Simpkins You shouldn't have come here. I hope neither of you has fallen in the stream.
Tom No. We took good care we didn't.
Nora We have samples.
Andrews I specifically ordered you, Nora, not to come here ...
Nora I said I was sorry, Father, but I had to do something.

Andrews moves towards Nora

I want you to stay over there, please, Father.
Andrews What? But why?
Nora Because ... I don't trust you any more.
Andrews (*dreadfully shaken*) Nora ...
Nora I want to make sure I don't drop this sample. I want it analysed. Properly this time.
Andrews Listen to me, Nora ...
Nora (*upset but determined*) No, Father, I won't listen to "good sense and reason". I want it analysed.
Andrews Nora, you must stop this nonsense ...
Nora Mr Simpkins. I want the sample properly tested this time.
Simpkins Try to be reasonable, Nora. Tom—can't you reason with her?
Tom I'm on her side.

There is a silence

Nora You all want me to be reasonable. Then I will be reasonable. I'm told that this water is not contaminated, that it's well known it's spring water from the mountain. If that's so then it's reasonable that I can drink it.

She puts the test-tube to her lips

Andrews No! Don't do that.
Nora Why not? It's perfectly safe. Reg didn't die because he swallowed some of this water. He died of natural causes.
Andrews Don't drink it, Nora.
Nora Why not?
Andrews Because ... we can't be sure ...
Nora That's why I want it properly analysed, Father.

There is a silence

Will you promise me, Father, that it will be done properly this time?

Andrews looks defeated

Simpkins I promise you, Nora. I'll see to it that it's done.
Nora That's all I want. (*Gently*) Father.
Andrews Yes?
Nora Will you forgive me?
Andrews I just want you to come home, out of this place. We'll have to work something out ... Are you coming?
Nora Yes.

Nora and Andrews make their way out

Tom Come on Susan. Let's get out of here. Coming, Mr Simpkins?
Simpkins Call me Ted.

They exit

CURTAIN

FURNITURE AND PROPERTY LIST

Scene 1

Personal: **Mr Simpkins:** test tube with dirty water
Susan: caving helmet and torch

Scene 2

Personal: **Mr Simpkins:** torch
Susan: torch and helmet
Tom: torch
Reg: torch

Scene 3

Personal: **Mr Simpkins:** large map

Scene 4

Personal: **Nora:** letter
Susan: petition and pen

Scene 5

Personal: **Nora:** letter in pocket

Scene 8

Personal: **Simpkins:** one chair
Susan: one chair
Tom: one chair
Nora: one chair

Scene 10

Set: Telephone SL and SR

SCENE 11

Strike: Telephones

Personal: **Tom:** test-tube with water samples, torch
Nora: test-tube, torch
Andrews: torch
Simpkins: torch
Susan: torch

LIGHTING PLOT

Property fittings required—none

SCENE 1

To open: General lighting

Cue 1   **Simpkins:** "... we'll be off"   (Page 4)
Fade to Black-out

SCENE 2

To open: Darkness

Cue 2   **Simpkins, Susan, Tom** and **Reg** enter with torches   (Page 4)
Bring lights up faintly to give effect of caves

Cue 3   **All** exit   (Page 7)
Black-out

SCENE 3

To open: Lights full up

Cue 4   **Simpkins:** "Oh yes."   (Page 13)
Black-out

SCENE 4

To open: Lights full up

Cue 5   **Nora** exits   (Page 15)
Black-out

SCENE 6

To open: Lights full up

Cue 6   **Nora** exits   (Page 17)
Black-out

SCENE 6

EFFECTS PLOT

SCENE 2

Cue 1   **Tom** "... high-minded reasons"   (Page 6)
Heavy splash

SCENE 10

Cue 2   **Andrews** dials   (Page 24)
Telephone ringing

MADE AND PRINTED IN GREAT BRITAIN BY
LATIMER TREND & COMPANY LTD PLYMOUTH

MADE IN ENGLAND